JOHN RUTTER
LONDON TOWN

A CHORAL CELEBRATION

FOR MIXED AND CHILDREN'S CHOIRS, WITH PIANO

London Town was commissioned by Children's International Voices of Enfield, in celebration of the 80th birthday of their founder and conductor June Keyte. It was composed in 2018 for performance by Children's International Voices, together with primary and secondary-school choirs from the Borough of Enfield. Grateful thanks are due to the Enfield Residents Priority Fund for their support of the project.

MUSIC DEPARTMENT

OXFORD
UNIVERSITY PRESS

OXFORD
UNIVERSITY PRESS

Great Clarendon Street, Oxford OX2 6DP,
United Kingdom

Oxford University Press is a department of the University of Oxford.
It furthers the University's objective of excellence in research, scholarship,
and education by publishing worldwide. Oxford is a registered trade mark of
Oxford University Press in the UK and in certain other countries

ISBN 978–0–19–352838–3

Music originated on Sibelius
Printed in Great Britain on acid-free paper by
Halstan & Co. Ltd, Amersham, Bucks.

LONDON TOWN
A Choral Celebration

JOHN RUTTER

1. Prologue: The Bells of London
(all choirs)

Words by Delphine Chalmers
(Bars 5–23: traditional rhyme)

*The split between younger and older voices is optional – if preferred, all children can sing bars 5–23 throughout, or sopranos and altos from the mixed choir can sing the two portions designated for older children.

OXFORD UNIVERSITY PRESS MUSIC DEPARTMENT, GREAT CLARENDON STREET, OXFORD OX2 6DP
The Moral Rights of the Composer have been asserted. Photocopying this copyright material is ILLEGAL.

A Same tempo, ♩· = 72, with a feeling of swinging like bells

kiss,____ We toll____ a toast____ to hap - pi - ness.____

kiss,____ We toll____ a toast____ to hap - pi - ness.____

kiss,____ We toll____ a toast to hap - pi - ness.____

kiss,____ We toll a toast to hap - pi - ness.____

On the shrill wag - ging of our clap - per tongues____

On the shrill wag - ging of our clap - per tongues____

On the shrill wag - ging of our clap - per tongues____

On the shrill wag - ging of our clap - per tongues____

sound the a-larm for fire,___ war and plague In-to the star-less

sound the a-larm for fire,___ war and plague In-to the star-less

___ the a-larm___ for fire,___ war and plague

___ the a-larm___ for fire,___ war and plague

night._____ Cus-to-dians___ of Lon-don's streets, We

night._____ Cus-to-dians___ of Lon-don's streets, We

In-to the star-less night.___ Cus-to-dians___ of Lon-don's streets, We

Cus-to-dians___ of Lon-don's streets, We

13

Our cheeks blush bronze at the

Our cheeks blush bronze at the

Our cheeks blush bronze at the

Our cheeks blush bronze at the

Measure 151. Soprano, alto (mf, dim.): "Vi - vos vo - co, mor-tu-os plan - go,"
Tenor, bass (f, mf, dim.): "vi - vos vo - co, mor-tu-os plan - go, vi - vos vo - co, mor-tu-os plan -"

J Measure 159. *rall. al fine*
Soprano (mp, dim., p dim., pp): "vi - vos vo - co, vo - co."
Alto (mp, dim., p dim., pp): "vi - vos vo - co, vo - co."
Tenor (dim., p dim., pp): "-go, mor - tu - os plan - go."
Bass (dim., p dim., pp): "-go, mor - tu - os plan - go."

2. London Zoo

(children's choir)

Words by John Rutter

The gi-raffes have quite an e-le-gant air, stroll-ing here and there,

But the e-le-phants car-ry a heavy load, They lum-ber a-long on the

jun-gle road; And down in the grass the

cob-ras crawl, But I real-ly don't like them at all, So I

run and watch the kan-ga-roos hop, Lick-ing my ice-cream fresh from the shop. I

wave to the mon-keys and stare at the bears, Feel sad for the pan-da with no one who cares;

Then I think to my-self rid-ing home on the bus:

Do *they* get bored just look-ing at us?

3. Mind the Gap

(*all choirs)

Words by Delphine Chalmers

*Children's choir to join in at conductor's discretion where appropriate.

Text © Delphine Chalmers 2019.

Hurt - ling back-wards in our seats,_____ We're tap-ping out a time - hop two - step:_____ Mind the

gap and feel the beat, feel the beat,_____ feel the

SOPS and ALTOS

beat,_____ feel the beat.

FULL CHOIR

B SOPS and ALTOS

Ra - cing down the Ju - bi - lee Line To South - wark in six - teen - o -

-nine_____ We watch ruffed ac - tors play the round on

long white knu - ckle nights. The Bard may tug his beard in fright But

wis - dom will shine through: Our des - ti - ny___ is in our hands —

To thine own self be true. Change here for the

46 North - ern Line For Lon - don Bridge and burn - ing lime. **FULL CHOIR** *mf* We hear the whip - snap

50 screech of fire___ *f* Tear down Pud-ding Lane._____ **SOPS and ALTOS** *mf* The Thames is trem-bling at the

54 flames, **FULL CHOIR** *mf* But Lon - don will be saved: The bu - ckets passed from

58 hand to hand *f* Prove hard - ship can be braved. **SOPS and ALTOS** *mf* So next we're

speed-ing down the Ba-ker-loo Line; We reach two-two-one B in time To glimpse the slink-ing sleuth in search of clues in cob-bled lanes;___ He rat-tles off his tight-lipped quips, His an-swer is spot on:___ 'Al-ways trust your in-stincts — E-le-men-t'ry is

poco rall.   FULL CHOIR **E** **Slightly broader**
𝅘𝅥 = 132

how   it's   done.'_____   But   when   we   reach West-

-min-ster   In the spring of nine-teen-for-ty-five   We   see   this   is   a   ci-ty   That a

blitz   could   not   de-stroy.   One   voice   of   the   na-tion   Has

brought   the   coun-try   to   its   feet;   We   kept   the   home   fires   burn-ing   Till   the

day when there was peace, there was peace,_____ there was

peace,_____ there was peace._____ And as we

steam in-to King's Cross The en-gine breathes a sigh; We hear the cries of bust-ling por-ters:

Plat-form nine-and-three quar-ters!_____

4. Lines written in the Tower of London

(mixed SATB choir only)

Words by Sir Walter Raleigh

5. The River's Tale
(tenors and basses)

Words by Rudyard Kipling (1865–1936)

"I walk my beat through Lon-don Town, Five hours up and sev-en down. Up I go till I end my run At Tide-end-town, which is Ted-ding-ton. Down I come with the mud in my hands And plas-ter it o-ver the Map-lin Sands. But I'll have you know that these wa-ters of mine Were

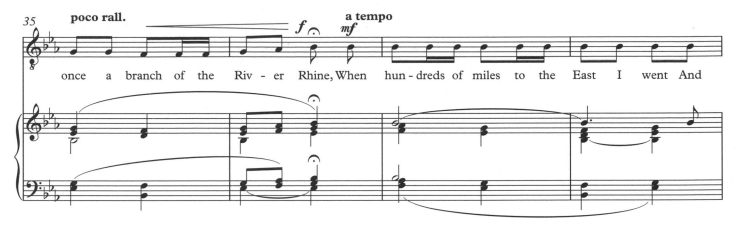

once a branch of the Riv - er Rhine, When hun - dreds of miles to the East I went And

Eng-land was joined to the Con - ti - nent. I re - mem - ber the bat - winged

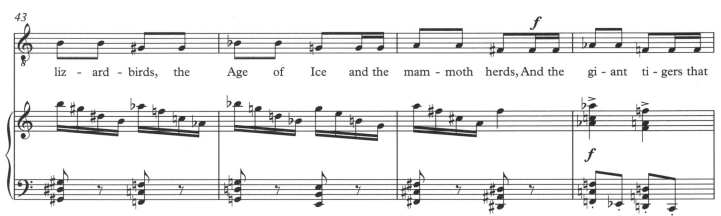

liz - ard - birds, the Age of Ice and the mam - moth herds, And the gi - ant ti - gers that

stalked them down Through Re - gent's Park in - to Cam - den Town.

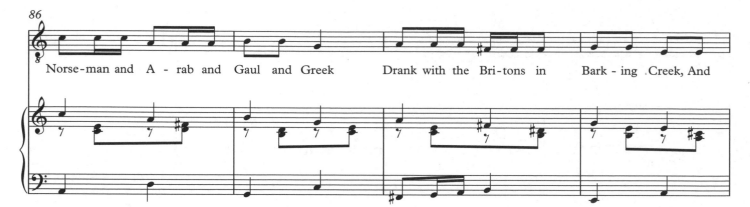

Norse-man and A - rab and Gaul and Greek Drank with the Bri-tons in Bark-ing Creek, And

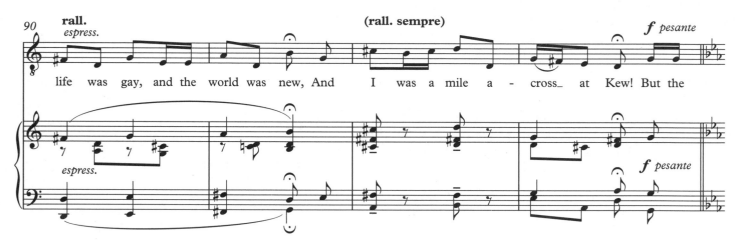

life was gay, and the world was new, And I was a mile a - cross at Kew! But the

Ro - man came with a hea-vy hand, And bridged and road-ed and ruled the land, And the

Ro - man left and the Danes blew in– And that's where your his-to-ry books be - gin!"

6. Finale and epilogue

(*all choirs)

Words: William Wordsworth

*Children sing their designated portions from bar 81 alone, but can also join in elsewhere at conductor's discretion.

can-dle-light? Aye,_____ and back a - gain.

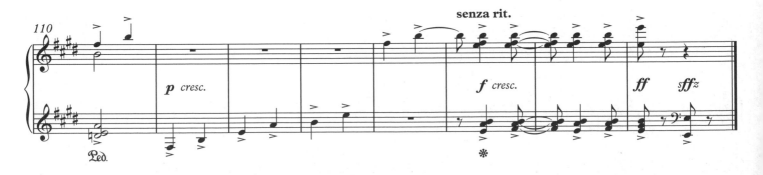